The Good Girl
is Always
a Ghost

The Good Girl is Always a Ghost

Anne Champion

Black
Lawrence
Press

Black
Lawrence
Press

www.blacklawrence.com

Executive Editor: Diane Goettel
Book and Cover Design: Amy Freels

Copyright © 2018 Anne Champion
ISBN: 978-1-62557-800-6

Published 2018 by Black Lawrence Press.
Printed in the United States.

CONTENTS

I. STAGGERING BLOOMS

II. THE MOST TERRIBLE THING

III. ONLY OUR BONES OBEY BY BREAKING

IV. SHORT BIOGRAPHIES   85

"In what way are you different? Are you saying there haven't been artist women before? There haven't been women who were independent? There haven't been women who insisted on sexual freedom? I tell you, there is a great line of women stretching out behind you into the past, and you have to seek them out and find them in yourself and become conscious of them."
—Doris Lessing, *The Golden Notebook*

I. STAGGERING BLOOMS

WOMAN KNIGHT OF MIRROR LAKE

For Qiu Jin

> "Don't tell me women are not the stuff of heroes."
> —Qiu Jin

Don't tell me that mountains don't form under our tongues and plunder
air,

    our voices can't clatter ears and force blindness into sight.

I'll take the dagger into me before I'll take a man.

    In my sleep, the gauze turns my bound feet to concrete

and every step bashes the earth to wreckage, the cracked terrain

    wrinkles into canyons and craters, hidden paths for my sisters to
    follow.

My skin collects scars like wildflowers plucked from a garden,

    the dirt writes and rewrites, and I welcome the collisions of fists

and knees and elbows, the dented metal armor, bruising a body

    that never wanted shelter. When men speak of women, they
    forget

how our bodies are the first map in which they became lost.

I lift the swords of the dead and drag them in my wake,

carving a bladed future in the dust, so lucid that I know—

they'll aim the blade at my voice. The sword is the last thing I'll
see.

ANNIE OAKLEY

Yes, I said it and I'd say it again: a woman
should be just as comfortable cradling a gun
as she is swaddling babes. Why? Because a woman
can be trusted in ways men can't. I'm sharp—
if I wanted to shoot the ash off a man's cigarette,
I could. If I wanted to shoot off his head, I could do
that too, but I'm a lady so I'd ask first. Not politely,
just matter of factly. Those men sit around shuffling
cards, placing bets on chance, but I can swipe
their Ace of Spades, fling it in the air, show them
the holes in their lives. Did you know when I began
they put me in the circus? The circus! A woman
with a gun is like a bearded lady or clown.
And they did laugh, they squirmed in their seats a bit,
especially men, but when women squealed
it was only at realizing they could save themselves.
I always said women should get their own brigades,
that wars could be more effective that way—tempered
with good sense and empathy and wit, and let me tell you:
when a woman's pissed her aim is *perfect*.
We don't falter, not like those lizard-skinned lawmen
shedding chunks of scales every which way and not like
those teenage pimple pocked soldiers who come back,
spirit broken or deranged. I tell you we could do it.
I'm not just a Wild West show. I married a man
but I birthed nothing but bullets.

INDIRA GANDHI SPEAKS TO NIXON

It's unpleasant, talking to men about war—
like a visit to the gynecologist, when you want
to ask, *Is there a woman I may speak to about these matters?*
But I am stuck with him, quipping about
the gray streaks in my hair, joking
about Frankenstein's bride, and I say, yes,
Mr. President, I was not made by God:
a political woman is always made by man.
Don't think I don't know what a man like him
says about me behind closed doors.
He'll call me a witch, maybe worse,
but witch is my favorite. If only
I had such power—I'd curse them,
give them all vaginas and let them fumble
as they try to rule with such a handicap.
To see Nixon in a dress, his looks under careful
scrutiny, what a fantasy. I admit it,
this is what I think of every time
we meet. I stare at the wall and imagine
Nixon painstakingly applying lipstick
to meet with me and I think,
Not this old hag again, nagging about Russia.
It's a shame we have to run the world this way,
under the fists of men with egos so frail
they start a war. Nixon will call me
a cunning fox, he'll say I suckered him again,
but we're both cursed: he'll ruin himself,
I'll rely on men to protect me from ruin,
and we know how that ends for a woman.
And when the men who loved me grieve

my death, they'll shed blood and not tears.
I scribble in my notebook, never meeting his stare,
and his voice finally stops, waiting
for me to fawn at him, and I look up:
How much longer must we speak, sir?

THE HILTON CONJOINED TWINS

Beauty isn't pain, as they always told us.
Pain is pain. We longed for the man swallowing
fire, doodled his last name in our diaries,
and when our bodies blossomed, every man
we beckoned with our bouquet of fingers was him,
snuffing out the flame in his stomach,
pulling it back reignited—men
were nothing short of magic,
and we dreamed ourselves into a double dip
strawberry cone. Beauty isn't pain.
We looked so delicious
in our plump, starched petticoats,
a giant cupcake, two dollops
of frosting on top in the shape of bows.
Later, the smudged black eyeliner,
the flapper girl fringe, the knee-high boots—
two bad girls in cahoots, whispering
and waltzing behind whorls of smoke.
We sang of heartache with shrill, trilling
chickadee notes but didn't know the first thing
about loneliness. It was all an act:
children begged for pictures, men demanded
we lift our skirts, show precisely where we're glued.
Only pain is pain: the steep bank of skin
between hip bones, our four tangled legs, gliding
into spotlights double-wide and innocent eyed.
And curtseying—the tent trembled and purred
with applause. Beauty is not pain.
We tried to marry, but every judge called us indecent,
incestuous. Secretly, they wanted to watch us:

who could condemn a threesome forced
by God? When the curtains fell, when our manager
ran off with our money, when the drive-in
movies replaced the stage, only then
did we daydream about cuts—when one
would slice her finger on the grocery bags at work,
we'd look at each other in awe. It could be so gentle,
a swift slice of skin. Scalpels dangled over our sleep
like baby mobiles over a crib, metal clangs
soothing us to sleep. When one of us starts
to vomit, the other sings jazz:
The show is over. The curtain is descending.
We know that when one of us dies,
the other will bear her like an anchor
until she pulls us both under.

BETTIE PAGE AND THE WISDOM
OF OLD AGE

The world's worst sin is shame,
     and the punishment for it is women.
God didn't tell Eve to hate her body—

     He gave her air baths in Eden, a figure
that undulates like a river. I know
     girls are trying to recreate me;

I've seen them in the magazines, backlit
     by men's craving. I know the ways
they deflated to bones, the forced withering

from girl to good girl. The punishment
     for shame is us: we torment men
as our hour glass curves expire.

They need us so they want to see us
     bound and gagged. They love us
so much they have to kill us. I know

     the click of a camera is the same
language of the fist, the beating tempo
     as you strip and pose, the skin's petals

unfurl submissively for every flash.
     Young Betties, turn your wrists
to the lens, reveal the map

of your blue veins, stun
with your pulsing defiance, refuse
        the shame that wants you tamed.

Now that I'm near death, I can
        tell you how the six men pinned
me to the concrete, and I knew

        enough to say *harder.* I can
tell you that my daddy's name is a cut
        in my cheek that reopens

with every forced smile. Once,
        there was a boy who loved to see
me gagged and he died from watching.

        On my wedding night, my husband
wrapped his hands around my neck
        and said he'd finish me for good,

but God intervened. And then God
        and the Devil never let me rest,
fighting over the damned in my earshot—

        even a mythical man is still a man.
Don't listen to the lessons for the good
        girls: have no shame, ignore

the posture poses, the arrangements
        of fine china, the curtsies, the closed knees.
Learn the body's trapdoors, how

to make steam rise from your eyes,
that even your spine's arch is a flirt,
and that love is impossible

with the heart of a girl next door—
it's temporary, like a child's tooth,
its root will weaken: it'll be swallowed

or spat out. My body vanished and will soon
vanish again. The good girl is always a ghost,
and her body is always a gash.

"DIEGO AND I" (FRIDA KAHLO, 1949)

My love for Diego is as deformed
as my spine. I'd like to say it holds
me up, stirs the doughy batter
of my body into a cyclone
of a woman taunting a man
with her full skirt and Jarabe dance.
No, it's a crushed and crooked thing
I can't live without. I've always been a bitch.
I've always been a painter.
Diego made me better at both.
Every time he touches me, he knows
my body is a desert, my feverish skin,
my landscape, fine sand
that grows nothing, but still
he toils, and I baptize
our babies in my blood.
Do you know what it is to love a man
who can turn a wall into sky,
who can make a heart into a wall?
My paintings are not transformative—
there's nothing surreal in them.
Diego is inked on my skin.
Diego is my third eye.
Diego's third eye is an eye
that wanders like his other
two eyes. And Diego makes
me so female that my hair grows
into a noose. Like a man,
he watches. Like a man, he needs
his hands to kill me. Like a man,

he can set my body aflame
without a match, crush me
into pieces like a puzzle, like the trolleybus
did, my first accident. And Diego,
my second, who hammers nails
into my joints and I split open
like a cadaver on an autopsy table.
This is as real as it gets.

MAE WEST INSTRUCTS HOW NOT TO LOVE

Look away from the platinum crown;
it's not a message. It doesn't say
I'm the "come upstairs for a good time" gal.
It doesn't smell of strawberries
left in a kitchen sink; you don't need
to hover over me like fruit flies
or dance yourself into a frenzy
around a streetlamp. Keep that up
and I'll love you the way wet hair clings
to a girl after a hot bath—a little cold
and brittle by morning.
You don't need to hold me
like a spiked punch bowl ready
to splash onto your pristine carpet.
Don't ogle me like nipple tassels
you confuse for fireworks
in a bourbon blur—
if you keep looking at me like that,
I can only take you like a bullet.
I'm not a woman like the rest,
but I'm a woman nonetheless.
Love me right, and I'll love you
more than my pen as it pours
across the page characters
so brazen that I can hear
the censors' black pens snuffing
out every breath. I'll love you
like the cross-dresser loves makeup,

loves the blisters that heels leave on his toes.
I'll love you with the tenderness
two women take to bed
when they can sneak away
from their husbands and kids. I'll love
you like the pianist can't admit
he loves the out-of-tune key—
how he learns to make it work
in a song, how he never gets over
the surprise of it not sounding
exactly how it should.

DEAR MARILYN MONROE

You didn't teach me how to be beautiful; you exposed
what the world does to a beautiful woman when everyone starves
for her, when you have no choice but to let them feast
on your body. The only thing they desire
more than your silhouette is a woman's romance
with self-destruction—a body like a charred
tree trunk, the crooked limbs, the bareness
of a self that's blackened and brutal.

People tell me I'm beautiful too—adoration pierces
me like darts in a mound of clay. I know the men that catcall
wouldn't care if my eyes were replaced with shimmering marbles,
my skin with smooth plastic, my insides, gouged out
and hollowed, because beauty crowns like halos.
I watched them watch you, Marilyn, and I'm afraid.

JOSEPHINE BAKER ON HOW SHE DID IT ALL

I'm a Freudian's daydream: one twirl of my banana skirt
could set them spinning like tops, dizzy with penis envy

and sexual repression. I envy no penis—the audience
needs every beautiful woman adorned

with a crown of phalli around her sex. It's a tilt-a-whirl,
a kind of hypnosis. Getting naked is the perfect

camouflage for a woman. Once they see your tits,
they'll never see you as anything else. The great

disappearing act. A nude woman is a joke,
and laughter stings like a branding iron until

no one will suspect you of anything. I drank
with Nazis and hid Jews in my house. I left lipstick

prints on cigarettes and left enemy secrets
in invisible ink on my sheet music. Don't forget:

jewels are armor. They get so distracted
by something shiny. The female torso is a weapon;

it slithers like Eve's temptation. Men and women
fell into my snare and I shed my skin, rose

from the ash of my sex, so that when I died,
they marveled and recoiled in equal tempo,

My God! She was everything!
She was *everything.*

AFTER THE ATTIC

"It's a wonder I haven't abandoned all my ideals, they seem so absurd and impractical. Yet I cling to them because I still believe, in spite of everything, that people are truly good at heart...When I look up at the sky, I somehow feel that this cruelty too shall end, and that peace & tranquility will return once again."
—Anne Frank, *The Diary of a Young Girl*

After the attic, I awoke
and realized my heart was a nest, and
that all hearts are this way, places of refuge
to harbor eggs we name

and nurture, until hope hatches
and squawks with insatiable hunger.
My nest is slipshod: broken twigs,
dirt, and dust motes, but others

have nests made with silks,
gold fillings, human hair. Some
are dug from a hole in the ground.
The dawns have changed;

they wake me like a hammer on a skull.
The sky used to hold such promises.
My birds are starving. They want worms,
but here there are only mice. And I am weak,

I can feel the twittering of old ideals,
beaks agape, waiting to be fed,

but I have nothing to give.
They hatched too soon

and will never fly now. I used to dream
of flight—when I held my pen,
I thought I was soaring.
When Peter kissed me, I believed

nothing could ever hurt again.
I remember, but my vision has blurred—
when I see cigarettes, I think of chimneys.
I try to evoke happier thoughts: the thrill

of a gumball machine—the turn, the pop,
the surprise, the vibrant color.
Yesterday a young girl was shot.

                                    Pop, then red.
My nest is unweaving. I can't
                        hold these

jittery, shifty
            creatures anymore. Last night,
                                    Margot fell
from her bunk.
                She smacked concrete,
died from shock.
                        I have been ill.
                                    I looked up
        at the sky today,
                    and the stillness of clouds

    are gray statues

of mythological beasts.

Sister,
    little bird,
        I will follow you soon.

NICKNAMES FOR WILMA RUDOLPH

As if by magic, your older sisters transformed,
a scent trailing them, candied blood and iron,
making the boys yowl at them like police hounds.
You knew this couldn't be your fate, so you unlocked
the metal braces, stayed after school and ran
the track for hours, because it felt like an infinity
you could measure. It must have ached at first, the rusty
limits of your joints, your newly unveiled skin
gasping like a newborn, all while the rest of your body
was blooming like the dandelions
splitting the dirt and pock marking
the lawn. At school, you learned names:
every country, every species, every type of rock.
Which plants are toxic, which flowers
to slip behind an ear. I imagine your teachers
never uttered the names for dark skin,
never taught you where they came from,
because you knew it in your veins; you could
deconstruct your pulse to know when
one meant lynching or one meant anomaly.
We called you The Tornado,
and you must have known we were afraid
you could destroy every foundation we've known.
We called you Black Gazelle, and you must have felt
your fangs grow, nourished by anger, hungry
to rip out the gut of the world that set
the records to break. The ones who admired
called you Black Pearl, stressing
how rare you were, how valuable, adorning
you around their necks for special occasions, proof
that Jim Crow didn't clip wings. You ran—

You ran until your bones felt brittle, until your muscles
wrapped around your skeleton like vines.
Whenever you crossed the finish line, did you re-learn
the futility of escape, that the track goes and goes
but the laps are only a temporary stay
against your permanent world?

PLEASE TELL ME THIS ABOUT HELEN KELLER

The first woman I remember
whose story was meant to be a lesson:
Stop complaining. God is real. Rise above adversity.
What I saw was a person double cursed:
woman and disabled, damsel and victim.
You learned to turn touch into letters
and it was a miracle that they didn't leave
you trapped in your head like the madwoman
in the attic. But what I really wanted
to hear is that you knew the way the trees bruise
and then shed all their colors like dead skin.
Not that you saw it, but that you felt it,
as true as a heartbeat. I wanted to hear that once
you touched someone's lips to listen to him,
but there was no alphabet for desire.
That his lips met yours and you saw
the way bark glows before flame chars it.
I wanted to know that he wanted
to marry you, and you saw the fall's red leaves
as they wailed at you like a clanging alarm,
and you knew—that the trees were doing this
all your life, going skeletal for winter,
but always inflating again with buds and bloom,
that he ran his fingers through your hair and coaxed
you into colors you glimpsed in kaleidoscopic dreams.
Tell me that he truly saw you.
Tell me they didn't force you to be a saint.

FLORENCE NIGHTINGALE: THE LADY WITH A LAMP

Isn't it strange that angels are female, crowned regal by halos of gold,
    swinging lamps to peel the darkness away

from wounded men? You'd think something so powerful must be male,
    but I've seen what men are made of,

scooped out and sawed off, and I tell you, they're nothing but matter,
    disposable, easily lost, just like us.

They litter our rooms with uniforms and weapons that call them back
    into my memory.

Harold asked me to kiss his forehead before bed at night.
    Thomas cried for his mother.

Henry said I was his angel but he didn't know the blade meant life.
    Every day, the news is the same:

I'm losing another man I'll never know. It's not the men proposing
    marriage, not my father's stern commands

that I fall in line with my lot that haunt me. It's the men I can't save.
    Nurses aren't a flock of angels—

they're herded power, a way to say, *See what I can create out of ruined parts.*
    I watch my shadow drag at my heels,

a sleepless woman; the wounded men see something more.
My body, pivoting in their hallucinations

of more life, can't be seduced. Women, understand this glowing
creature I can make of you—

someday, you'll wake in a bed so stiff, you'll think it's a casket
and you'll wish you knew the magic

to heal. Don't hang your lamp outside that door; no light illuminates
those creaky, boarded houses.

ANNE SEXTON PREPARES FOR THE END

After the shoulder heave of a garage door,
    my feet press into slippers, an unseemly weight.
        In the rearview, my skin's a little sagging—

it's no secret time is erasing me,
    and only vodka can wet my thirst.
        I inhale its pungent punch,

the scent familiar in its knock-out
    discomfort, just as my body is only
        familiar when the knots squeeze

like hangman's rope. No one said
    the end would be so hard, like swimming
        against a current, collapsing into the masonry

of death. I've always imagined I'd die
    flaring up like a moon flower, face gasping
        towards the glow, body nestled in dirt

like tenderness. While driving, people
    stop looking human, as headlights
        smear chalk into a charred night.

The cars are always coming and always going.
    Endings have always felt like hallucinations
        or assaults to me. Impossible to differentiate.

I tell you, this life has never been
      mine. Do you feel it? The dissolving, the thrust
            of daily waking, fatigue trailing like a shadow,

each step quicksand inhaling you like a no-good lover,
      like the weight of my mother's old fur coat,
            like always choosing the paths along the cliffs,

adrenaline junkie, shameless flirter with death.
      When I'm gone, they'll pilfer my poems
            to trace the trash of my days. In the car,

the engine hums my final cry, the air tastes as rich
      as dollops of frosting on a wedding cake;
            I turn my face to the sky—dear night-

blossoming body, it's time to give the world
      your staggering blooms, it's time to cast your shadow
            across the moon, muted calyx tongues tasting grace.

II. THE MOST TERRIBLE THING

THE MOST TERRIBLE THING

For Sylvia Plath, on the 50th Anniversary of her death

Your imagination springs its jaw
on me like a rat trap, snare snapped
at the neck, tiny metal teeth
leaving a row of scars, and I
a smiling woman, seeking to loot
your treasures, sea of adjectives
in a dark, cold mud bath of declarative
muck, oh, little bloody mouths, oh,
fat gold watch. Oh, you—
you bewitched us, cursed him,
and set us all ticking in a trance
of engines, churning and turning
and burning for you. I pray
to you more than I pray to God;
I am your opus, your valuable
jewel, your daughter, living still
in a world too cruel, a life
you shrugged off like a heavy
winter coat. But I carry on
for you, my throat caressing
your syllabics as I ask the Ouija
to bless me in your name, recover
your voice amongst the fiercest flames
where the golden lotus still grows.
Your tragic romance—everyone thinks
they know; women kneel down
to kiss your boot in their face.
For years we've let your voice
sing. We need you to be
the most terrible thing.

AILEEN WUORNOS

"Thanks a lot, society, for railroading my ass."
—Aileen Wuornos' last interview

Every woman is born bound to the railroad tracks.
     Look, my hands in cuffs make angel wings.
          Look, little boys turn hands into guns or fists.

You assume male monsters are more recognizable
     than me: fucking bullshit. More easily forgiven, maybe.
          They walk among you every day, sniffing

at women's crotches like stray mutts, the attack
     always excused as provoked, as the nature
          of a dog. Think of your little girl,

all her life, you'll discipline her to softness—
     you'll ignore her canine teeth, you'll train away her rage.
          When I touched men, I choked back the bile of revulsion

until I learned how to touch flame without a burn, how to
     laugh in an unlit alley, how to wrench darkness
          from its comatose. Finally, I could look in the mirror

and fall in love with my anger, nursing power
     like a real mother. I lit a cig after every man I shot—
          smoke snaked across their corpses and lassoed

them. It felt like purity. It felt like orgasm.
     I'd coughed up that bone of alienation, choking
          feral dreams all my life, as I was kicked and kicking,

harnessed in cages and put down when wildness
turned rabid. Every woman is born strapped to a track,
the train is coming, and no one gives a shit about rescue.

I WISH THEY TAUGHT ME ABOUT LOZEN

Columbus Day, 2015

I loved the Native American women: their beads,
feather headdresses, long black hair like Cher.

We learned about exactly two of them: the women
who helped white men. But we imagined the others:

their brown bodies sinewy, fingerpainted, caressed
by white men, making the All American babies.

My dad called me his little Indian squaw when I tanned,
claimed my brown eyes were the Cherokee in me.

But everyone said they were part Cherokee.
I never learned the difference between truth and legend.

I never learned about Lozen, who scalped white men's hair
for bounties, who tamed the wildest horse

and could teach it to swim across a river
just by touching its mane and whispering in its ear.

I never learned how Lozen would spin with her palms
to the sun and wait for a tingle in the tips of her fingers,

pointing, *There. The enemy comes from there.*
They say she could even predict how many.

But who knows the truth from legend?
The enemy came from everywhere

and they were many. When the victorious wrote history,
they'd erase her like a smudge but ink Victorio and Geronimo.

Women still weave baskets and cradle
papooses and white men still point their guns at everything.

Last night I dreamt a white man came into my classroom
and pointed a gun at my head. I pulled his hair

until his neck rested on my shoulder like a baby.
He cooed like a man that needs mothering.

And if it'd been the real world, I'd have been dead.
And if it'd been the real world, I'd have been an angel.

But it wasn't, so I split his neck from ear to ear
until I could grip his spine like a flag pole,

stick his head in the ground and stake my claim.
I was Lozen. I am Lozen.

I know men and I know violence. I know
what's true and what's legend.

SADAKO SASAKI

In the hospital, the children breathe in sync.

                          The machines chirp out patterns of our pulses,

but we all hear a countdown. Hospital jargon

                          is a language we were never taught in school,

but the script of death is something

                          I've always known. I don't remember running

through the black rain of Hiroshima, the winged

                          air lifting me and tossing me out the window,

but I know it as surely as I know

                          that once I was safe inside a womb.

The adults know that diseases need

                          nursery rhymes and lullabies to soothe

them. But each story sets my heart twitching

                          like a dying bird. I read of a wolf

eating a girl whole and being cut

                          from its gut and rescued. But what if

the wolf is safer than the world? I hear

about a girl that begged the
gods

to escape a man and turned into a tree.

I shudder to think of being
rooted

in dirt, unable to flee from probing.

My mother counts my ribs,
each bone that keeps

me whole. My roommate counts too,

claims 1000 origami birds
will grant us one wish.

We tear out pages of newspaper, turn

each blotted headline into
wings.

We never read them: history

is the most dishonest myth.

We lose count—how many folds?

How many beaks? We fold
milk cartons,

napkins, glossy pages of Hollywood

starlets whose bodies have
hills and valleys,

a topography I know I'll never have.

I dream cranes come to life
and peck at my body.

I dream I turn to statue—forever a girl,

a legend, a lesson war-crazed
men never learn.

SALLY RIDE WATCHES THE CHALLENGER EXPLODE

I know what it is to be boxed in hot flame,
        ushered into more darkness, pinpricked
by the flamed needles of stars. All my life,

I carried the burdens of planetary panic.
        An engine propelled and shuttled me—
Do you cry when the job gets too hard?

No, but when The Challenger bursts
        and my friends turn into a firework display
of smoke, and everyone curiously coos

as if this must be the intended magic of space flight,
        my bones quake. My heart drums a beat
of onslaught. *Do you wish you were a man?*

I've been fighting long enough to know that men
        can't save me, and danger knows no gender.
When my friends die, I taste that gooey gel

we ate in space—it's stuck in the back of my throat.
        It tastes just like rage. Two women died.
Judith, whose weightless curls made a halo

that startled everyone. And the schoolteacher,
        who only desired to show her children
that there's a world outside of this world.

Did the flight affect your reproductive organs?
   We all want to shatter those G force shackles.
Today is doused, and tomorrow

is always a threat, an inescapable
   meteor collision. I'm alone
and my lover can't hold me in public,

because she's a secret I must protect
   from questions. I have only this:
my plump lungs, my empty stomach,

a match struck and held to my toes,
   fire blistering every part of me,
fire igniting my friends every day I wake;

I can't understand this machine
   of grief, its solitary gears,
its churning, its malfunctions.

CHRISTINE JORGENSEN SPEAKS TO THE PRESS

There are two things that make a man feel powerful:
a cock and a gun. I had both. No sir, I never tended
any gardens, never nursed any sons, never let a man love
me so hard that he beat me until I was bitter and wise.
There's one thing that makes a woman feel powerful:
love. Loving is wonderful, but falling in love
is very stupid. I don't want to marry—even though
men hover around like hummingbirds at hollyhocks,
I'll never let one move in. My religion is to never
put a wild thing in a cage. I wasn't really ever a man,
so I never sowed a field, sir, never liked the way
a football wanted to be cradled like an infant,
never listened when they told me you could plant
grenades in the earth and grow a great nation
full of heroic men. No, thank you, sir. Yes,
you may take my picture. No, I'm not Cinderella.
I never liked fairy tales because I don't like the myth
of the charming man. But the witchy woman,
she's real. I drink hard, I smoke hard, I do everything
to excess and it will make a man's clothes melt
right off his body. What do I say to those who laugh
at me, sir? You have every right to laugh, so long
as you can laugh at yourself first. Yes, I'm really sure
I don't want marriage—I didn't do this for the ragged
apron or the poodle skirt. Look, I don't need
a husband; I don't need to bargain
to get what I want. I know what you're going to write
about me: you're going to say I tossed off my Bloody Mary

like a guy. You're going to marvel at my hip-swinging
gait, my slim, trembling fingers, my girlish giggle,
my rosy blush. Not girl enough in one sentence.
Perplexingly girl in the next. I don't care. I can tell
you how to find paradise but you'll never write
it down: be who you are, don't be too bizarre,
expect very little from this world,
and don't be surprised when a woman
gives a revolution a swift kick in the ass.

ALBERT CASHIER

I knew I was a man when I wasn't afraid
to court danger, when I put on father's trousers,
walked out of father's house
and into myself. A war will turn boys
into men and blast women from their pronouns.
In battle, the earth reveals itself
as a mother masked by blood,
men's greatest uniform of war. I took solace
in the life of a man—I voted, I made my own money,
I worked with my hands, I was never pestered
about beauty and marriage. Even as a child,
I knew battle had little to do with war.
When they locked me in a mental institution,
my mind slid out of reality as easily
as I tripped on my skirt. When my hip
cracked on the floor, I remembered
scurrying up a tree to raise my company's Union flag—
sniper bullets soaring past my body—hanging the tattered
cloth to a high branch, thinking: *They will not get me.*
Even if the bullets penetrate me, they cannot kill the man.

SEARCHING FOR AMELIA EARHART

At age seven, I believed I would fly someday,
tramping through our house
in my father's leather jacket,
arms hanging limply to the floor,
and his old pilot's cap
with the smudged goggles from god-knows-where,
so big that they left indentations on my cheeks.

I sat on the stool of his workbench in this attire,
encircled by oversized dreams as he crafted
miniature model airplanes from World War I
and hung them from the ceiling,
tipped as if in mid battle.
Here, Earhart's mystery plagued us,
the films explored all theories
of her disappearance—the crash
on a deserted island, the love affair
with her navigator causing them to run away
with new identities, the capture by the Japanese
and the internment camp.
I can still hear her voice clearly,
feel its patient, whispery drawl
creep out of the television screen
and jolt down my spine like a zipper
coming undone:
We must be on you but cannot see you.
We are drifting but cannot hear you.
We are listening.

When I gave up the idea of flight, my father rescued
my poster of her, framed it by the workbench
alongside Lindbergh and Rickenbacker.
Her tranquil face, smooth and undaunted,
stared at me every time I grabbed my keys
and fled that house.

Still, even after so much time, I've never been able
to tell him that I never really gave her up,
not favoring her ability to fly anymore, but instead
her power to vanish.

INSOMNIA AND WINE MAKE JACKIE KENNEDY REMINISCE

Wooing oozed out of his pores,
and I'd been trained like a thoroughbred horse
to swoon with the command of a heel
in my side. My coyness leapt over fences,
all muscle and majestic grace. At first,
I never thought about how our romance
played for audiences. When we danced at balls,
his fingers could raise the heat up my spine
like mercury in a thermometer.
Loyal wife, expert at decoration, it was a role
I never had to audition for—I was a purebred woman.
I knew my way around a racetrack.
But the truths he didn't say were a fire
fanned by a flag at half mast. On nights
he didn't come to bed, I unbridled,
kicking in my stable. I dreamed I cried for help
but I was drowned out by applause.
I restored the house so we lived in a giant antique.
I turned us into a museum of myths:
it was so pleasant to revise us with a love story,
to reupholster the worn tears, to take down
the mirrors because we didn't need our reflection
anymore. I raised my children in that dollhouse, never cracking
my porcelain façade until I looked
down and bits of skull were in my lap.
Memory is like an old, delicate swath
of fine upholstery—a blood stain doesn't come out.

TO JUDY GARLAND

I think of you sometimes at night
while swallowing fistfuls of pills: sleeping pills,
vitamins, birth control, Xanax, anti-depressants.
Not exactly the sort you were married
to, but I look to them like wizards
that can bring me back home. I abuse
them too, large doses with a glass of vodka,
and, blissfully, they erase whole days.
Occasionally, I've been blessed with afflictions
requiring painkillers that sucker punched
me cold, wiping away nightmares
and heartaches like dust on a jewelry box.
I think of that character in *Valley of the Dolls*,
molded from your messes,
her desperate squeal: *Give me my dolls!*
All I need are my dolls! I recognize
how imperfection scorches, how every day we die
a little, how a voice can soar over rainbows
like a bird alighting a tree already in flames.
I have ruby red slippers I wore for a costume—
I admit, it's a kind of magic to don some sparkle,
but you need something to fill you
after the glitz is washed off or streaked
in rivulets of black mascara from too much
whiskey and too much confession to a bartender.
I've dated men made of tin or straw, skipped
with them over bright bricks and clung
to them in woods. They crumple with pressure,
they hollow you out. They can swipe
you from sturdy ground into sky;

they can make their voices boom
behind curtains until you tremble.
So, give us our dolls, I say, blot out the grief,
chase the fears away. Judy, before I sink
to sleep, I want to watch you tap dance tipsily,
trot across my hardwood floors,
and tell me that smoky command:
Come on, girl, get happy.
Keep all the demons at bay.

DEAR AMY WINEHOUSE

Dear bones and track marks,
Dear touches that make you almost detonate,
Dear flaking make-up and unwashed beehive,
Dear camera flashes like lightning—

Dear Amy, I don't remember you alive.
In magazine pages, you looked like my neglected
Barbies, hair impossibly tangled into rubber limbs,
plastic torso tossed into the black hole
of my boredom.

Dear Amy, sometimes life feels
like a never ending wake.

Dear bad influences, Dear
Jukebox on repeat, Dear marriage
like a grim reaper. Dear voice,

like jazz, they said, *like old fashioned blues.*
It was the ordinary blues that trailed you—
It will make you a ghost before it makes you a corpse.

Not jazz—a melody that snakes a pattern
no one can predict. Everyone predicted.

Watching the public watch you
was like watching a man blow up an inflatable
doll until it pops—her collapsing
breasts clinging to him through spit
and hot breath, and still
he gropes.

Dear lace bra peeking
through a tank top. Dear dangling
cigarette. Dear not giving a fuck
about anyone giving a fuck.

Dear kisses like scabbed knees,
bleeding with every scratch.

Dear Amy, you look beautiful
in the movie posters.

Death does that: polishes memory,
sands self-destruction into a smooth grace,
gifts a generosity that life
never granted, a perfect orb of sea glass.

LISTENING TO BILLIE HOLIDAY

Billie, it's like your voice rips off the seal
on my envelope of pain. My stories
pour out—at least I've finally reduced
them to alphabet, the way you molded
yours into melody and metaphor:

Southern trees bear a strange fruit,
blood on the leaves and blood on the root,
black bodies swinging in the southern breeze,
strange fruit hanging from the poplar trees.

I've always thought a piano sounded
a little like a pulse. I've always thought
a saxophone sounded like every hurt
I couldn't speak. I've always thought
jazz betrayed a truth no one wants to admit:

that we have no path, no map
to guide us, wayward and unruly,
we can't create a way out of loss—
the heart's dizzying mazes
and trap doors. Billie,

I know you died with track marks
on your arms that led to nowhere.
I know someone beat you,
someone raped you, that you had to
prostitute as a child, the forced abortion,
the Jim Crow humiliations, the cops
arresting you on your death bed—

the death of an icon leads to a public
autopsy of pain. But at night,
your voice undoes me—
brassy, unstrung, a solo
of breath hissing to be let in
through a crack in glass,
strange, bitter fruit,
swaying in the breeze.

EVA BRAUN, MISTRESS TO A MONSTER

Politics, such things are men's concerns.
The wolf loves me because I don't threaten
authority. The wolf loves me painted pretty

and demure—the weaker I am, the more
he loves. He's married to the country,
wants his sex symbol status to carry us

through the war. Sometimes he turns
from me for months, and this country becomes
a mistress I can't endure. I turned the pistol

to my chest and fired, and he saw how weak
I am, cradling me like a toddler. The country
never sees such tenderness. In public,

the wolf shuns me, and I trail him
like the breeze, taking photos for history
books. Do you know what it is to love

a man through a lens? He comes apart
from the world, his body yanked from reality
by the frame, and I swear it made me

more loving and more lonely. Sometimes
I ask him to teach me how to rule the world,
but he scoffs and says such things are men's

concerns. *A man never asks how to apply*
lipstick, so a woman should never ask
about men's business. He never spent the night,

never watched me put my lipstick on
in the morning; it's true he knew nothing
about women. But love, I taught him that.

Too late, perhaps, but he knew loyalty
when I pledged my life for him.
All those years, I wondered how to win

his love, and I learned I only had to be willing
to die. When I bit the cyanide, Hitler
didn't weep, but looked at me like a father

and said I'd finally learned patriotism
like a man. Life and Death,
such things are men's concerns.

NURSERY RHYME TO THE GIRL WHO WANTS TO GO INTO POLITICS

In the voice of Benazir Bhutto

Always carry lipstick and anti tear gas in your purse—
A woman with ideas is as good as cursed.

A chador can't protect the brain in your head—
The political woman is as good as dead.

III. ONLY OUR BONES OBEY BY BREAKING

EVA PERÓN

Don't ask me what they worshipped in this
    disintegrating body, my heartbeat like skipping
        stones across a lake. I used to love like a woman

        famished, take men like a slingshot, like the bed
    was nothing but sky without a trace of storm.
As a child, I had to wrench myself from a gangrene

lesion. Poverty helixed rage up my backbone
    that I twisted into my taut bun every morning.
        In the slums, the poor bellowed and yearned.

        I touched them to remember: I am no saint.
    But they stared as if I hovered in air. Hush,
I'll tell you the secret of a political woman:

Be as beautiful as an actress, as humble as a nun,
    open your legs to a political man and let thunder
        clap from your thighs. Die young. Let disease

        pluck at your body like a vulture until you transform
    skeletal like a nightmare trick. Or let a man kill you.
Either way, they'll clog the streets and embalm

your corpse into the nation's most beloved doll.
    My people, pray for this riotous heart, may rebellion
        be your weapon. Remember me whenever you exhale

smoke, the way it stings, the way it traces the air
and proves it's there, the way it threads retribution
into the rags you wear. Argentina, I'm always here.

I don't sleep. I don't suffer. I beg the streets with you
always, the tumors trailing my insides like a string of pearls.
Someday, this country will be a place where fire

doesn't birth cinder, where conviction refuses the master
and the chain, where hope is parched mouths kissing
a sky never charged with lightning, a cascade of merciful rain.

FASHION ADVICE FROM THE
COUNTESS

"Dress suitably in short skirts and strong boots,
leave your jewels in the bank,
and buy a revolver."
—Countess Markievicz

You were the Countess of Flight: revolt
is only the forced migration of time towards new trends.

A man thinks a woman's best accessory
is a set of rusted steel bars and impossible locks.

During your first arrest, you had a coin purse
full of bullets and a shoulder knocked

from its socket by the butt of a rifle. You didn't want
mercy. When the guards told you stories of brave

men who'd escaped, you looked them in the eye
wearing the same expression of flirtation

that you'd given the shy boys of your youth
and said, "I wish your lot had the decency

to shoot me." You donned a tiara to political meetings
and careened with men like a train, the impact

shook loose your sequins and diamonds,
replaced them with a gun and a knapsack of knives.

Even with your long arms and your steady aim
and your years of resentment fossilized into serrated rage,

you sought capture, you offered your wrists,
your neck, your chest—only to call their bluff,

that they lacked the courage to neutralize your threat.
At the podiums, with your sensible boots and words

unfurling into the air like expensive silk scarves,
you made all their jewelry rattle and sever:

the finest thing a woman can wear is her untethering.

MISSISSIPPI GODDAMN, [FILL IN THE BLANK] GODDAMN

For Nina Simone

They say violence never solved anything.
They say if you must resist,
you should forgive and ask nicely.
Violence will make you look savage, they preach,

and then they'll send your boy
a draft card and ship him off to Vietnam.
They'll call him a criminal
and lynch him from a telephone pole.

Your husband wrapped himself
around you like a snake, choking
the problem of love right out of you.
You said if you had a choice in this world,

you would've been a killer.
Freedom isn't about choice:
it's living with the absence of fear,
a feeling you've never known,

indescribable, like a girl who's never
been in love but swears by her fairy tales.
You said sometimes you felt free singing.
Sometimes you felt like they didn't know

you were already dead, it was only your ghost
clinging, hammering
at the keys, trying to transform pain
into action. Music was always in your head;

the more you played, the less you slept.
Blue pills to sleep, yellow pills to perform.
More pills to numb anger
that snapped like a broken bone.

At the piano, you fought the world.
After the applause, you fought yourself.
An artist holds a mirror up for truth,
and reflects a constant state of emergency.

America is a cancer that must be exposed
before it's cured, and you could only curse it.
Mississippi goddamn. Birmingham goddamn.
Los Angeles goddamn. Ferguson goddamn.

Your body was a tool, made by man, used by man,
abandoned by man, lying on your side, waiting
for a gust of wind to run through you like a flute,
so at least you could leave the world with a tune.

Baltimore goddamn. Charleston goddamn.
Staten Island goddamn. Cleveland goddamn.
_____Goddamn._____ Goddamn.
_____Goddamn._____Goddamn.

ROSA PARKS

My sister & I sat in some hole in the wall in Michigan.
A few patrons danced to country music & we were drunk

on cheap beer and high on our future plans to move to big city life
& Cathy asked the DJ to play Outkast & he said it wasn't that kind of bar.

"But Rosa Parks died today!" He nodded perfunctorily
& the speakers started vibrating & all the white people

sat down & we had the dance floor to ourselves, pointing
at the men on their bar stools and commanding them to hush their fuss,

as we shimmied our way to the back of an imaginary bus.
Cathy's skirt bloomed & I said "If I do anything

with my life and I die, I want people to celebrate!"
Dancing was always our secret revolt, blasting Jackson Five

when our parents weren't home, learning how to unblock the BET
    channel
& memorizing the lyrics to TuPac and Biggie. My best friend was a black
    girl

& I loved a black boy, so I knew I didn't want to be a racist like my parents
whose Confederate flag was the first thing to greet me every time

I walked in the door. We didn't know what we didn't know yet.
We were celebrating because we still believed the myth

that people could stand for something & the world would shift
& everyone was basically good. We didn't know that another girl

refused to give up her seat before you but she was a teenager & pregnant
& a black body needs undeniable sainthood to be granted compassion.

Maybe we thought it enough to simply not be racists.
I didn't anticipate that I'd always have to fight—did you?

Once I was walking down the street at night & I saw a black man
coming toward me & I felt afraid & when he got closer he reached his arms

out like he was going to grab me & fear singed my gut like a branding iron
& then I looked up and he was my former student,

reaching out to give me a hug. I always have to remind myself
to wake up & if I forget for a minute how this world was built on the backs

of black bodies then there's no hope. But sometimes now I don't know
about hope, Rosa. Did you hold onto it that whole century of your life?

Even through housing segregation? Even through the War on Drugs?
I know that freedom is a dream I was sold

& that the hero worship in schools for Black History Month
were sedatives for rage, because black bodies are still in danger,

& my friends will say they're not racist but when a black child dies
they'll say words like thug & debate the woes of the ghettos & forget

who built them, who threw the loaded dice so that they always win
& a cop never points a gun at them, & when I cry I know my grief

is real but I know it can't compare to the tangible pain of a mother
& I know you got the bus seat, eventually, & how long will it take

for there to be a space for everyone, not only to sit, but to be safe,
& what can I do to make that happen? The day you died we used our
    bodies

to dance & honor a symbol of justice & later we'd use our bodies
to march, to rally, to shut down the trains and the highways, to storm the
    police

stations & chant outside the prisons & we go home so weary,
but I know that racism means broken necks, cracked bones, bullets

tearing through flesh, & so long as I stay awake I can never sleep
without the nightmare of the real world on my conscience

& I miss the days when I believed enough in change
to just celebrate a hero & dance for her.

JANIS JOPLIN

Music is like making love
with a lover that doesn't spend

the night. He washes you off
before the moon clocks out,

and he fucks you the same way
fame does: furiously and other worldly,

a drug high, ephemeral guard
from the pressurized reality.

Once you have the talent,
the rest is all ambition,

and ambition is only a measure
of how badly you need to be loved.

The anger of men branded
me, but not without a hind leg kick—

they didn't recognize that I, too, am made
of pioneer stock, the stubborn mule

genes of Texas. I'd build an empire, turn
delirious in the face of the world's mutating

lies. With a crown of feather boas
clipped to the brown knots

of my hair, I trailed behind the crocheted
yarn of dying things, entered the maze

of glinting needles, fevered the kaleidoscopic
hallucinations of desire. I purged

the ridicules until they were androgynous
and mute. I never learned to bake

bread, but I knew how to be a star.
My gut was made of embers, my voice

rose and contorted like smoke—
it'll suffocate as it unmasks

this world in a single, throaty note.

OCCUPANTS OF VESSEL

An Erasure Poem from Harriet Jacobs' Incidents in the Life of a Slave Girl

time,   a walk out of doors,   the fresh air

revived.   human voice

a whisper.   recognize

my disguise.   I prayed

nothing.   Bring out his dagger.   We walked

seafaring

our secret.

We are only

occupants of   vessel.

I   remain,

hide

the vessel,

avail me.

The boat   rowed

to   swamp.   Snakes increased

venomous bites.   I dreaded to enter.

                    choose.   I   accepted

        my   persecuted friends.

SANDRA BLAND

I've never seen
a body lynched

from a tree

and I never saw
your body

hung by a garbage bag

in a jail cell. But
I don't see

much difference between the two.

HARRIET TUBMAN HAS A VISION
ABOUT THE FUTURE

America: she's going to get old
and her knuckles will fracture
but she'll never stop making a fist.

And then there'll be lightning
and it'll be white, blue, and red,
and it'll be the police.

And then we'll hear thunder
and it'll be a gun,
and it'll be black like America.

And skin will be armor only when it's white.
And black won't be camouflage, even as the sun retreats.

And then we'll feel the rain
and it'll be blood
on our hands.

And then we'll sow the crops
and it'll be the bodies
of dead black boys
we reaped.

And then everyone will pray
and the blacks will plead, please God,
and the whites will recite grace,

and if this is the prophecy,
then I've finally envisioned the skin colors
of your Father, your Son, and your Holy Ghost.

ELEANOR ROOSEVELT AND AMELIA EARHART SNEAK AWAY FROM THE BALL TO GO FLYING

We're giddy schoolgirls tonight, trying to fit into white pairs of gloves with swollen

joints and chafing skin, as if womanhood could be easy. *I feel like I'm in a costume*

in this godforsaken gown, Amelia quips. I feel like I'm in a costume whenever someone

calls me First Lady. Sometimes when people say President Roosevelt, I look

up, mistakenly thinking that's my name. I showed Amelia a clipping about Lindbergh

and said, *Look, it's Gentleman Earharty!* Can you imagine the indignation of men if they

had to wear the names of women as penance for their ambition like we do? Amelia

and I trip on our gowns climbing into the cockpit—it's not the champagne, it's that

gender is always a clumsy performance. *You think we'll be missed at the party?* Amelia

asks. I think we're decoration, a couple of balloons, contorted into animals

in the calloused hands of men. When I take the stick to steer the plane, moxie

knocks the wind out of me, I swallow the copper taste of freedom. Earhart says her

wildest goal is to circle the world.

Mine is to save it.

QUEEN BESS ON HER LAST STUNT

In all my schooling, no science of aerodynamics
could explain why gravity pulls harder

on a girl like me. I needed to defy it.
When Hollywood called, I thought maybe

the lights would finally illuminate
the girl they saw as shadow. But they told me

to don tatters, hold a walking stick,
and wear a pack on my back. Instead,

I barnstormed, teased gravity
with every figure eight, every dive,

barely missing their heads. I used to go to bed
imagining they still felt me in their wind stroked

hair. I never mistook a cloud for an eclipse.
I never mistook an eclipse for permanency.

But history swallows people like black holes,
and that's what I was thinking of, when I last

leaned over the cockpit to observe the terrain:
how miniature everything could become,

how less imposing everything looks
from a god's eye view. Then gravity wrenched

me from the machine that freed me
and took me back. I tell you, *I soared.*

CONVERSATIONS IN WHICH NICOLE BROWN SIMPSON'S GHOST APPEARS

Your blood turned to ink
smudging the tips of our manicures,

the details of your death paraded
our living room, erased the daily soap operas.

My mother says: *She was nearly decapitated.*
A death like that can only come from a man who loves you.

It's as if I put my hand in your corpse
and found myself caught

in a snarl of vines. The lawyers
and the litany of a battered life,

the letters, the stalking, the rapes,
the beatings, the threats.

A crime of passion, they say.
A violence that's domestic, they say.

Domestic, like your dog that nudged
your bones, licked the puddles of blood,

and barked for help. Years later,
my therapist says: *He breaks in through*

your window in the middle of the night
and you think you've never been loved

like that before? Have you heard
of Nicole Brown Simpson?

For months we're combing through
your crime scene, the caterpillar

crawl of justice. Every woman
watching had no need for proof,

the threat of a man is in our DNA.
My boyfriend says:

With domestic violence, you always
have to question how it was provoked.

My student says: *Oh no, he'd never*
go that far with me. We have a baby.

Before the verdict, your framed
face flashed across the screen again,

I saw it and remembered the way
a girl's tongue razes falling snow,

the way her heart grows roots
after her first kiss, the way

a woman's smile
can be a muzzle.

WHAT PRINCESS DIANA TAUGHT ME

That the first betrayal
always comes in the form of a kiss.

That a man doesn't need his hands to cast
shadow puppets on your wall.

That a man's wandering eye
always adds ten pounds.

That you can purge what nourishes you
but you can never purge what doesn't.

That a woman who isn't virginal
is no kind of mother.

That it's better to be nobody's
mother and nobody's wife.

That you can never divorce
your body.

That a camera is a serial killer
that targets young women.

That tears have more value
than jewels in a crown.

That he'll never leave his wife
even if he's already left his wife.

That a woman scorned is more adored
than a princess bride.

That a body can collapse delicately, like satin,
for the world to fold and unfold forever.

FOR MEENA KAMAL

The wildness of women can't be plucked like papery moth wings.
Your police batons are a firebrand, and only our bones will obey

by breaking. One after another, each of us gulps the Afghan air
and butterflies the desert with our sanded voices. This is not rage:

this is a recitation of an ancient prayer. Come closer and listen—
I want to tell you a story of blood and men and castles

resting on human remains. It is centuries old with the usual lures:
shadows of women lurking in bare margins, sleeping lions erupting

after being prodded by sticks in the ribs. It's a heavy tome
that steadies like an anchor. Every woman knows it by heart.

For my country, I'll give my open throat, and from it, I'll strip
the begging from their mouths, dowse them in the sweat of tulips,

their bodies rewritten through blossom,
their pollen-stained faces turning toward the sun.

IV. SHORT BIOGRAPHIES:

Josephine Baker: American-born French dancer, singer, actress, and first black woman to star in a major motion picture. She is noted for her contributions to the Civil Rights Movement and for assisting the French Resistance during World War II by acting as a spy. She married four men but was bisexual.

Benazir Bhutto: First female prime minister of Pakistan and the first female leader of a Muslim nation. She was assassinated during a campaign rally for re-election as she stood up to wave at the crowds through her sunroof. Shots were fired and explosives detonated, killing approximately 20 people. On the day she died, she had lipstick and homemade anti tear gas liquid in her purse.

Sandra Bland: Bland gained national attention in the United States after she was found dead in her jail cell, hanging by a plastic bag. Bland was pulled over for a failure to use her turn signal and subsequently arrested. Bystander video footage revealed that the officer asked her to put out her cigarette. She asked him why, and he told her to get out of the car because she was under arrest. She questioned what he was arresting her for, and he tried to drag her from her seat and threatened to use his taser. He forcefully threw her to the concrete and shoved his knee in her back before putting her in handcuffs. After this video was released, more questions arose from community activists regarding her death; many suspected it wasn't a suicide. Others argued that even if it was a suicide, the police should be held accountable both for the unlawful nature of her arrest and for the neglect of adequately monitoring her in jail. However, there were no indictments for Sandra Bland's death.

Eva Braun: Adolf Hitler's secret mistress. Braun attempted suicide twice, generally interpreted as cries for Hitler's attention. She served as his professional photographer, though he never acknowledged their relationship publicly, not wanting to tarnish his sex appeal with the general public. Braun often called Hitler "the wolf," a play on the meaning of Adolf— noble wolf. Before his death, Hitler married Braun in a secret ceremony, and they committed suicide together. Hitler gave both Braun and their dogs cyanide pills before shooting himself in the head. They were married for 40 hours.

Albert Cashier: Transgender Union soldier during the Civil War. Until the age of 17 years old, Albert lived as Jennie Hodgers; he changed his full name and gender identity when he left home and enlisted in the 95th Illinois Infantry in 1862. Albert died in a mental institution suffering from dementia at age 71: he was forced to wear a skirt, which led to a broken hip due to him being unfamiliar with wearing women's clothing, having lived his entire adult life as a man. His hip never fully healed and he died shortly after.

Bessie Coleman (Queen Bess): First female African American pilot. In order to make a living, she performed as a barnstorming stunt flier. She had a reputation for being flamboyant and skilled, stopping at nothing to perform difficult stunts. She was once asked to be in a movie, but she pulled out of the project once she realized her character had racist and stereotypical characteristics. Coleman died at 34 years old when practicing for a stunt that required a parachute jump. She leaned over the cockpit to examine the terrain, and the plane dived unexpectedly—she was thrown from 2,000 feet in the air and died instantly when she hit the ground. It was later discovered that there was a wrench jammed in the gearbox of the plane.

Amelia Earhart: American aviation pioneer and author. Earhart was the first female aviator to fly solo across the Atlantic Ocean and she broke many other aviation records. During an attempt to fly around the world in 1937, Earhart disappeared, and her aircraft and remains were never discovered, despite costly and intensive search efforts. This poem references the last words that were heard over the radio from Earhart before her disappearance.

Anne Frank: Jewish German-born diarist and writer, famous for her WWII diary, *The Diary of a Young Girl.* Frank was forced to go into hiding to escape Jewish persecution during Hitler's regime, but she was discovered and transported to a concentration camp. Anne and her sister Margot died of typhus in Bergen-Belsen shortly before the camp was liberated. Witnesses testified that Margot fell from her bunk and died on impact from shock. Anne died a few days later.

Indira Gandhi: First female Prime Minister of India. She served from 1966-1977 and again from 1980-1984. She had frigid relations to the United States, with Nixon secretly referring to her as "that old witch" and a "clever fox." On her part, Gandhi often could not hide her disdain for world leaders she disagreed with. In a meeting with Nixon, she appeared visibly bored, and she finally interrupted him to ask how much longer they would be forced to speak. Gandhi was assassinated in 1984 by two of her Sikh bodyguards, which prompted a violent response in the form of the 1984 anti-Sikh riots in which 2,800 Sikhs were killed by mobs.

Judy Garland: Singer, actress, and vaudevillian. Garland is most remembered for her role as Dorothy in *The Wizard of Oz,* though she had a long career and international stardom. Despite her successes, she had much turmoil in her personal life, and she struggled with drugs and alcohol, ultimately leading to a fatal barbiturate overdose at age 47. This poem references the book and movie *The Valley of the Dolls,* the main character of which is rumored to be modeled off of Judy Garland.

Billie Holiday: African American jazz musician and singer-songwriter. Holiday has a tumultuous bio; she was raped, worked as a prostitute at age 14, endured violent relationships, abused heroin and alcohol, and faced flagrant racism. She died from cirrhosis of the liver due to drinking, and she was handcuffed in her hospital bed as she lay dying while her room was raided for drugs. This poem references her song, "Strange Fruit," about the lynching of black people in the south. The song was first written as a poem by a teacher, Abel Metropol in 1937.

Daisy and Violet Hilton: A pair of British conjoined twins born in the early 1900s. They were exhibited as children, and they toured the U.S. as sideshow, vaudeville, and burlesque acts in the 1920s and 1930s. They last performed in the 1960s, and their managers abandoned them, penniless. They ended up working in a grocery store. They died a few years later of the Hong Kong Flu. Daisy died first, Violet following a few days later.

Harriet Jacobs: African American writer who escaped slavery. Her book *Incidents in the Life of A Slave Girl* was one of the first books to address female slaves' struggle for freedom. In this book, Jacobs speaks out about sexual harassment and abuse endured by female slaves and the difficulties they faced when trying to protect their children. She was an abolitionist speaker and reformer.

Qiu Jin: Chinese revolutionary, feminist, poet, and writer who was executed in 1907 after a failed uprising against the Qing dynasty. She is considered a national heroine in China. Her marriage was unhappy, and she left it, abandoning her two children to study in Japan. She was known to wear Western male attire. She returned to China to join the revolution. During her public speeches, she advocated for women's rights, including the freedom to marry, freedom of education, and abolishment of the practice of foot binding. She was executed by beheading and immediately became a symbol of women's independence. Her name translates to "Woman Knight of Mirror Lake."

Janis Joplin: American singer-songwriter of the 1960s, often known as "The Queen of Psychedelic Rock." Joplin trailblazed a space for women in rock music, though it should be noted that many of her most popular songs were originally recorded by black musicians that she admired. Growing up in the 1950s, she was severely bullied for her looks and her nonconformity, once voted by a group of frat boys as winner of the "Ugliest Man" contest. She was also bullied for her liberal ideas, specifically in regards to racial equality, and her clash in values with her Texas community led her to seek freedom in California where she pursued music and fame. Some sentiments in the poem are taken from her personal letters and public interviews. Joplin struggled on and off with alcohol and heroin, and she was found dead in a hotel room at the age of 27.

Christine Jorgensen: First American trans woman to become widely known for having sex reassignment surgery. Jorgensen served in the army during WWII, and her gender change attracted a significant amount of press. She worked as an actress, singer, and nightclub entertainer, and she was known for her bluntness and intelligent wit. Some sentiments in the poem come from her interviews.

Frida Kahlo: Mexican painter, known for her self portraits. Kahlo married Diego Rivera, a communist known for his political murals. Due to Rivera's infidelity, their relationship was tumultuous, and Kahlo had many affairs of her own with both men and women (including Josephine Baker). She suffered a bus accident as a teenager which led to health complications her entire life. Much of her art explored her personal pain in relationship to her body and her love of Diego. Though she was known as a surrealist painter, she asserted that her paintings weren't surreal, as they were autobiographical. This poem is an ekphrastic poem about her piece "Diego and I."

Meena Keshwar Kamal: Afghan revolutionary political activist, feminist, women's rights activist, and founder of Revolutionary Association of the Women of Afghanistan. She's considered the founder of feminism in Afghanistan. She believed that imposed illiteracy on women, the ignorance of fundamentalism, and the corruption of political leaders for financial gain were the cause of the immobility and oppression of women. She has a famous quote in which she refers to Afghan women as "sleeping lions," waiting to be awoken to fight for revolutionary change. She was assassinated in 1987. Her assassins were never caught, but it is likely that they were members of the government's intelligence service or secret police. Her husband was murdered a year before her, and the whereabouts of her three children are unknown. Tulips, mentioned in the poem, are considered the national flower of Afghanistan.

Helen Keller: The first deaf-blind person to earn a Bachelor of Arts degree. Keller became famous through books, plays, and films about her life, primarily through *The Miracle Worker,* which focused on her teacher, Anne Sullivan's, triumphant ability to break through her isolation and teach her language. Helen Keller went on to do so much more than simply communicate: she was an author, an activist, and a lecturer. She was prolific and outspoken about her convictions, fighting for women's equality and labor rights, while condemning the destructive exploitation of capitalism. She was a proud socialist and a stunning political thinker. Little attention is paid to her romantic life: in her 30s, she fell in love with Peter Fagan and became secretly engaged. She tried to defy her family by eloping with the man she loved, but ultimately she was unable to do it, due to societal attitudes that condemned sexuality and disability.

Lozen: Skilled Apache warrior and prophetess, sister of Victorio and warrior for Geronimo. It was said that Lozen could hold her palms to the sky and feel tingles that would tell her which direction the enemy came from and how many there were. It was also said that she had a way with animals, able to comfort horses that were anxious about crossing water. She was considered a fierce warrior in resisting European colonization.

Constance Markievicz: Known as Countess Markievicz, an Irish Sinn Fein and Fianna Fail politician, revolutionary nationalist, suffragette, and socialist. She was the first woman elected to the British House of Commons, though she refused her seat there. She was also one of the first women in the world to hold a political cabinet position. She participated in the armed revolt of Easter Rising and was arrested and sentenced to death. However, due to her gender, the court converted her sentence to life in prison. Upon hearing the news, she said, "I do wish your lot had the decency to shoot me." After being pardoned for this, she was jailed several times for her speeches and support of women's rights and her involvement in the Irish Civil War.

Marilyn Monroe: American actress and model, arguably the most iconic Hollywood actress of all time. Monroe's curves and platinum hair gained her fame, often forcing her into roles of unintelligent, materialistic girls. In reality, Monroe was well read, intelligent, and introspective. She had affairs and relationships with public figures. She died of a drug overdose, possibly intentional, when she was 36 years old.

Florence Nightingale: British social reformer, statistician, and nurse, credited as the founder of modern nursing through her efforts emphasizing sanitation during the Crimean War, which significantly lowered the death count. After the war, she opened a nursing school, which created a legitimate career path for women. Despite her efforts for women's equality and freedom, many scholars highlight a letter as proof she was anti-woman, in which she claimed that women's craving of sympathy made them not equally capable as men. She resented the lack of women enrolling in her schools and decried women's rights activists that advocated for female careers when women weren't taking advantage of the profession she'd created for them through her school. "The Lady with a Lamp" was first coined by a newspaper and later popularized in a poem about her by Henry Long-fellow. Nightingale is thought to have remained a virgin her entire life; she eschewed marriage because she thought it would interfere with her career and she felt that nursing was a calling from God.

Annie Oakley: American sharpshooter and exhibition shooter. Her talent led to international fame, and she often performed for royalty and heads of state. When she began, she performed in the circus. The line in the poem "A woman should be just as comfortable cradling a gun as she is swaddling babes" is attributed to Oakley; she also publicly expressed believing that women should have their own war brigades. Oakley married, but she had no children.

Jacqueline Kennedy Onassis: First Lady of the United States and wife of John F. Kennedy. She captivated the public as a fashion icon of the 1960s and her televised tour of her restoration of the White House was widely watched and helped create a favorable image of the Kennedy administration. As first wife, she devoted herself to hosting social events. She was present during the assassination of her husband, and she famously stood beside Lyndon Johnson as he took oath with her husband's blood on her dress. She compared her marriage and White House years to mythical Camelot, though her marriage was plagued by Kennedy's philandering.

Bettie Page: Iconic pinup model, nude model, and bondage model of the 1950s. Despite Page's image of unabashed sexual liberation, she experienced much strife: her father molested her; she was gang raped by six men in New York City; and she had several marriages, one to a man who nearly beat her to death. She was also required to testify at an obscenity trial after a teenage boy accidentally killed himself while looking at her bondage photos. After modeling, Page disappeared into obscurity. She became a born again Christian with hopes of doing missionary work, but she was denied the opportunity because of her divorces. Later, she began to hear the voices of God and the Devil speaking to each other. After a confrontation in which she stabbed her landlord over 20 times, Page was diagnosed as paranoid schizophrenic and institutionalized for nearly a decade. Page didn't allow herself to be photographed or interviewed on camera in her old age; she also refused to attend social events. She claimed she didn't like the way she looked and she wanted people to remember her as she was in her photos.

Rosa Parks: Civil Rights activist credited for beginning the Montgomery Bus Boycott by refusing to give her seat up to a white person on a segregated bus. Parks is often thought to be the first person to do this, but Claudette Colvin preceded Parks by nine months, and it was actually her court case that led to the Supreme Court ruling that made bus segregation unconstitutional. Due to Colvin being a teenager and pregnant by a married man, Civil Rights leaders felt that she wouldn't garner enough public sympathy, and they used Park's incident in campaign efforts for the boycott; Parks was in her 40s and married, and these details, along with the often repeated myth of how tired she was that day (she has stated that the only thing she was tired of that day was the way things were) was enough to give her iconic status in the movement. She dedicated her life to activism work, resettling in Detroit due to her notoriety in the South, but finding the housing segregation disturbing. She sued Outkast for using her name in their song without permission, and the case was settled six months before her death. She died in 2005 at the age of 92.

Eva Perón: Second wife of Argentine president Juan Perón and First Lady of Argentina until her death from cervical cancer at 33. Perón was born in a middle class family and moved to Buenos Aires to pursue acting before she met Juan. During his presidency, she became a champion for labor rights, she founded and ran charities for the poor, and she was outspoken about women's suffrage in Argentina. She also founded and ran the nation's first large scale female political party. After her death, the streets were congested with mourners for days, and her body was embalmed and put on display for public viewing.

Sylvia Plath: American poet and writer. Plath is best known for her semi-autobiographical work, *The Bell Jar,* which details her suicide attempt, institutionalization, and electric shock treatment. She also became famous for her poetry collection, *Ariel,* which was written the final months of her life: she's responsible for popularizing the confessional mode of poetry and for her unflinching portrayal of depression. Plath married Ted Hughes, whose infidelity led to their break up and caused Plath to spiral into another debilitating depression. She died by suicide at 30 years old.

Sally Ride: American physicist and astronaut. In 1983, Ride was the first American woman to travel to space as a crew member. She also served on the committee to investigate the Challenger explosion. Prior to her first space flight, she was subjected to sexist questions by the media as much of their attention focused on her gender. After her death, her obituary revealed that she'd had a female partner for 27 years.

Eleanor Roosevelt: American politician, diplomat, activist, and longest serving First Lady of the United States. In her later career, she devoted herself to championing human rights causes, serving as First Chair for the UN Commission on Human Rights and oversaw the drafting of the Declaration of Human Rights. Roosevelt had a close friendship with Amelia Earhart, and during one presidential ball, the two ran off together in their gloves and gowns to take a ride in Earhart's plane. Earhart let Roosevelt steer the plane, as Roosevelt had a keen interest in learning to fly.

Wilma Rudolph: American track and field sprinter, considered the fastest woman in the world in the 1960s. She competed in the 1956 and 1960 Olympic games and became the first American woman to win three gold medals in track and field during a single Olympic game in 1960. Additionally, she was a civil rights and women's rights activist. Various countries had different nicknames for her, including The Tornado, The Black Gazelle, and The Black Pearl. At age four, she contracted polio, scarlet fever, and pneumonia and grew up wearing a brace on her right leg. She shocked everyone when she removed the brace and walked unassisted at age nine. She was the 17th of 21 children.

Sadako Sasaki: A Japanese girl who was two years old when the American atomic bomb was dropped near her home in Hiroshima. When the bomb fell, she was blown out of a window; her mother ran out to find her alive and unharmed. They fled, but were caught in the black rain. In 1954, Sasaki was diagnosed with leukemia due to her exposure to the radiation and given a year to live. While in the hospital, her roommate told her of a legend that anyone who folds a thousand origami cranes will be granted a wish, so Sasaki began folding paper cranes. It is unclear if she ever made her goal, but she certainly folded hundreds of cranes, using any scrap of paper she could find. She died when she was 12, and her classmates folded a thousand cranes and buried them with her. Statues of her holding a golden crane are in the Hiroshima Peace Memorial Park and the Seattle Peace Park.

Anne Sexton: American poet known for her personal, confessional verse. Sexton started writing at the suggestion of her therapist, and she wrote poems about depression, mania, sex, womanhood, relationships, affairs, and motherhood. She won the Pulitzer Prize in 1967 for her collection *Live or Die.* In 1974, she committed suicide by carbon monoxide poisoning—she put on her mother's fur coat, removed her jewelry, poured a glass of vodka, locked her garage, and turned on the engine of her car. She was 45 years old.

Nina Simone: American singer, songwriter, pianist, and Civil Rights Activist. Simone was originally trained in classical piano, but began singing in night clubs to make money to support her family. As she garnered more attention and fame, much of her music began to address Civil Rights issues, such as her famous song "Mississippi Goddamn," which was a response to the Birmingham, Alabama church bombing that killed four black children and the murder of Medgar Evers. She became close friends with the Civil Rights leaders of the era, rejecting the notion of nonviolent revolt, advocating instead for an armed revolt and a separate black state. She was brutally beaten by her husband (also her manager), and she eventually left him and moved to Liberia. Her temper and violent outbursts along with her depressive and suicidal moods finally led to her diagnosis of bipolar disorder. She died of breast cancer in 2003. Much of this poem is comprised of paraphrases or direct quotes from her interviews or letters.

Nicole Brown Simpson: Ex-wife of professional football player O.J. Simpson. She was killed in her home along with her friend Ronald Goldman. Nicole suffered years of domestic abuse and stalking from O.J. Simpson, and her murder was particularly gruesome: she was stabbed multiple times in the head and neck, and her neck wound was so great that her larynx could be seen and her vertebra was incised. Her body was found after her dog's wailing led the neighbors to follow the dog, who guided them to her body. O.J. Simpson was found not guilty, despite overwhelming DNA evidence which linked him to the crime. O.J. Simpson later went to prison for armed robbery; he was released in 2017.

Princess Diana Spencer: First wife of Charles, Prince of Wales, eldest son of Queen Elizabeth II. Diana divorced Charles due to infidelity. During the marriage, she suffered anorexia, bulimia, and depression. She controversially exposed the secrets of the royal family by doing television interviews and secretly communicating with a biographer. She was killed in a car crash while being chased by paparazzi.

Harriet Tubman: African American abolitionist and Union spy during the Civil War. After her escape from slavery, Tubman assisted others to freedom using the Underground Railroad. She often had visions due to a traumatic head injury she received as a slave; she believed these visions were prophecies from God. Part of this poem is a rewrite of a quote she said at the beginning of the Civil War: "And then we saw the lightning, and that was the guns; and then we heard the thunder, and that was the big guns; and then we heard the rain falling, and that was drops of blood falling; and when we came to get the crops, it was dead men that we reaped."

Mae West: American actress, singer, playwright, and screenwriter. She is generally referred to as a sex symbol. Her entertainment career spanned over seven decades, and her work was well ahead of its time in championing sexual liberation, gay rights, and transgender visibility. Note: I use the term "cross-dresser" in the poem, which I'm aware is out of date, but it was the term that West often used, and the terms "transgender" and "drag queen" weren't used during this time period.

Amy Winehouse: British singer and songwriter. She died at 27 years old from alcohol intoxication. Before her death, she experienced significant paparazzi attention and tabloid rumors. A popular documentary about her life was released after her death.

Aileen Wuornos: American serial killer, often designated as the first female serial killer to be both classified as a sexual predator and to kill strangers. Wuornos was a prostitute who killed and robbed seven men. She first claimed that she killed out of self defense, because the men she killed were either trying to sodomize her or beat her. She later retracted that defense, but claimed in interviews that she only changed her story to ensure she'd get the death penalty as quickly as possible. Regardless, Aileen Wuornos lived a tumultuous and tragic life—her mother abandoned her when she was six months old, and she was raised by her grandfather, who was also thought to be her father. At 13, she was impregnated by a neighborhood pedophile, and she gave her child up for adoption, but she was banished from her house. She had to live in the woods at the end of her street, and she survived through prostitution. She briefly married a much older man, but she left the marriage due to domestic violence. Eventually, she met a woman who she lived with for three years as a romantic partner, and this was the time period in which she began to kill and rob the men that picked her up for prostitution. She was sentenced to death, and she was the 10th woman that the U.S. executed via the death penalty. At the time of her death, it was clear that she had an unhealthy mental state; many believed she was a paranoid schizophrenic.

ACKNOWLEDGEMENTS

Grateful acknowledgments to the editors who published the following poems, sometimes in slightly different forms:

Apt: "Diego and I" and "Please Tell Me This About Helen Keller";
Boxcar Poetry Review: "The Hilton Conjoined Twins";
Broad! A Gentlelady's Magazine: "To Judy Garland";
Eleven Eleven: "For Meena Kamal" and "Woman Knight of Mirror Lake";
The Fem: "Albert Cashier";
Fogged Clarity: "Searching for Amelia Earhart";
The Greensboro Review: "Mae West Instructs How Not to Love";
Heavy Feather Review: "Anne Sexton Prepares for the End";
Midway Journal: "The Most Terrible Thing";
Muzzle Magazine: "Bettie Page and the Wisdom of Old Age";
The Pinch: "Annie Oakley";
Pittsburgh Poetry Review: "What Princess Diana Taught Me";
So to Speak: "Aileen Wuornos" and "Sally Ride Watches the Challenger Explode";
Southword Journal: "Eva Perón";
Sweet: "Florence Nightingale: The Lady with the Lamp";
Up the Staircase Quarterly: "Conversations in which Nicole Brown Simpson's Ghost Appears"

"The Most Terrible Thing" won 2015 Best of the Net.

"Nicknames for Wilma Rudolph" and "Christine Jorgenson Speaks to the Press" appeared in the *Anthology of Forgotten Women* published by Grayson Books.

"Indira Gandhi" appeared in the *Nasty Women Anthology* published by Lost Horse Press.

Gratitude to The Barbara Deming Memorial Foundation for their generous grant that helped fund the writing of this manuscript.

THANK YOU

As always, thank you to my fellow poets. To Sarah Sweeney: your creativity and ambition inspire me always. To Ron Spalletta, Matt Summers, Dax Bayard-Murray, Francine Rubin, Liz Bury, Grace Schauer, Linwood Rumney, and Mary Kovaleski-Byrnes: thank you for your feedback, your camaraderie, and your friendship.

Special gratitude to the Colrain Poetry Conference for help shaping this book and giving me the confidence to continue forward. Extra thanks to Ellen Dore Watson for the warm encouragement towards these poems.

To Edmund Campos, Jenny Sadre-Orafai, Laura Watson, Catherine Champion, Matt Iwanowicz, Brittany Arneson, Ruth Baumann, and Kristina Marie Darling: there are no words for how much your continual support means to me. Lots of love to you all.

Thank you to the Barbara Deming Memorial Grant for Women for believing in some of these poems enough to help fund the completion of the manuscript.

Love to my father, who was the first to tell me stories of adventurous and accomplished women who broke gender constraints.

Anne Champion is the author of *Reluctant Mistress* (Gold Wake Press, 2013), *The Good Girl is Always a Ghost* (Black Lawrence Press, 2018), and *The Dark Length Home* (Noctuary Press, 2017). Her poems have appeared in *Verse Daily, Prairie Schooner, Salamander, Epiphany Magazine, The Pinch, The Greensboro Review, Thrush Poetry Journal, New South*, and elsewhere. She was an 2009 Academy of American Poet's Prize recipient, a Barbara Deming Memorial grant recipient, and a 2015 Best of the Net winner. She currently teaches writing and literature at Wheelock College in Boston, MA.